THE ROOM

OTHER ALEF BOOKS

* Suzanne Ehrhardt, *Threads*
Jeffrey Gustavson, *Nervous Forces*
Ilya Kutik [tr. Kit Robinson], *Ode: On Visiting the Belosaraisk Spit on the Sea of Azov*
* Melissa Monroe, *Machine Language*
Carol Moldaw, *Taken From the River*

---

* forthcoming

THE ROOM

JOSEPH LEASE

Alef Books
New York

The author wishes to thank the editors of the following journals, in which these poems first appeared:

Agni: "Higher Ground," "Petition," "Words like Rain"
The Boston Review: "But You," "I Can No Longer Live by Thinking," "The Night I Met Sue She Told Me This"
Colorado Review: "New World," "Orient Point," "The Sun Threshes, Seed Rains, A Cord of Wet Wood"
Grand Street: "Footloose radish . . . ," "Hammer," "Marathon House," "The Room"
The Paris Review: "Crystal Rock"
Pequod: "Michael Kohlhaas"
Southwest Review: "The Sun Drench"

"Michael Kohlhaas" also appeared in *Representation and Desire,* edited by David Shapiro (*New Observations* 43). Several of these poems appeared in a series of artists' books, collaborations with the painter Richmond Burton and the book artist Jonathan Hammer.

Published by Alef Books,
Box 563, Fort George Station, New York, NY 10040

Library of Congress Catalog Card # 94-71039
ISBN 1-882509-04-8

SECOND PRINTING

Cover by Richmond Burton.

This is the second book
in the Alef Series
of Poetry and Translation.

CONTENTS

HAMMER

Snow, rain, sun, nails.
Your hometown called sleep.
Your house in the sun
Shall have black cloth walls.
You wear black day after day,
Mourning the house.
Broken, fateful, cold.
Snow, rain, sun, nails.
What you fear came true
Years ago.
Families fill and empty.
The house you build,
The lead sun.
Snow falling straight down
On graphite-colored water,
Yellow slick leaves, concrete.
Gaze: one smile that
Hides nothing,
Promises nothing.
Families empty and fill.
Because.

THE SUN THRESHES, SEED RAINS, A CORD OF WET WOOD

Each step jiggles green hedges.
Violet, blue wind covers
River light, birches.

Slick mossed roots cup a rain
Pool; nurturing, your throat holds
Cadences and unhampers song.

Spend an afternoon's silver,
Drying rain, wood
Stacked in radiant sunlight;

Ground squishes. Air
Lightens; unmoving, cigarette butts,
Leaf shreds, float.

Sun opens an hour,
Sandstone, a blue rag.
You come home and laugh,

Buoyant as two hawks,
Sun-warmed, ordinary; a nourished
Clarity sings. A slow,

Reliable embrace, mud-slick, salty.

PETITION

Goldstein changed his name to Guston,
Liskofsky to Lease. You choke on signatures
Ancestors forged. Passport: sun and moon,

Apples, fish; no one will kill you.
Because nothing punished us
Everything became pleasure.

Culture: where you hang your name,
Cough up vodka, broken legs
Heaped on a floor, Poland, teeth.

A child swallows a mirror,
Begs for good love, kisses a big
Volleyball, likes crystal meth,

Stands onstage breathing the sour
Pleasure, no longer wanted.
Like prayer, a storm starts.

His house made of paper, drain clogged by hornets.

THE NIGHT I MET SUE SHE TOLD ME THIS

My father died when I was eight. The time right around there is totally closed, but before that and after that everything is so clear.

My brother and I were talking about this. My mother's attitude—my mother's attitude is like, "Couldn't you guys have picked something easier to do? Something more normal?" She loves us but she doesn't understand where we got this craziness. Why we're artists.

But she used to do things like wake us up at two in the morning so we could all watch "Twilight Zone" together. Or make us stay home from school and spend the day playing with her.

During my early childhood my mother didn't work. She stayed home to take care of us and we had our own little society. We're artists because of her. She still has so much imagination. Of course we got our craziness from her.

One morning my mother gave me a bath in the sink. I remember that. It's easier for mothers to give really little kids baths in the sink. My mother had a bad back and she didn't have to bend over as much. She just plopped the kid in the sink right in front of her.

(Sue looks down to the side and gestures—fanning open her arms.)

I can remember sitting in the sink like this. I remember how big the sink was around my hips. I moved around. What the water felt like. I remember how the dishwashing liquid smelled.

(She laughs.)

We had our own little society with our own values and rules. My mother read to us a lot. She read dramatically. She read things that really mattered to her. Not the way adults usually read to kids.

My father was a journalist. That might have been part of the reason why I wanted to read. My mother married my father when she was twenty. She quit college to get married.

My father really terrified my mother and my brother and me. He was a schizophrenic. I have clear memories of my mother and my father screaming at each other. And my father slamming my mother's head against the wall. Maybe it was the refrigerator door.

I knew how to read when I was two: nobody believed me—I used to read aloud and they thought I had memorized it.

BUT YOU

Glass moon pressed in the
Eye of the inexpressive dark green hill.
Marred foundations of water and air.
I go out to mail you a letter:
The only building that doesn't
Trace the progress of hyacinth in the stars
Wasting in flight.

WORDS LIKE RAIN

You think the words light rain covers a field and when you close your eyes for a second you are standing in a field, in the wet gray air, and you feel the rain on your skin. When you say the words light rain covers a field you pray that something will happen but nothing does because nothing can. Light rain covers a field. In an apartment across the street the woman is grating cheese for her salad: yellow pepper, tomato, cucumber, and purple cabbage sit sliced on red-leaf lettuce in the teak bowl. A cup of black coffee sits on the kitchen table. Her sister will come over soon for dinner; they will eat and listen to music and talk. Outside it's getting cold and if you don't have someplace you really want to be you wish you did because it's cold, suggesting the beginning of winter in New England, suggesting that this winter, when you have to go anywhere, the streets will trap you in a mouse-maze of painful cold, suggesting that you will need to buy a sweater or two that you don't have the money for. You hope at least that you'll get a phone call from a friend who wants to talk for a long time, so that you can bring the phone near the bed and get under the comforter and talk. Outside it's getting cold, colder than you would expect after such a warm afternoon, when people were lying on the grass reading in the sun. Cars go by in the street and as their headlights cross over you you think the people driving are hurrying off to be somewhere warm. People step out of the cold night into the supermarket. In front of the supermarket a woman talks to a man and near them a dog is chained to a bicycle rack. In the bar where you stop to get a slice of pizza to go one of the two guys who own the used-book store is watching basketball, talking about basketball. Who wants to be fifty and no health insurance, no family, no house; but it looks like that's the way things are heading.

MICHAEL KOHLHAAS

undisturbed was the first word,
the first metaphor, the
first moral

the first visual arrangement

there was never a first narrative,
no first ambition

but the classical plugs of light
and snow
and the tightness of mud
rings, and undisturbed glass
resting on your fingers,
the evergreens and ferns

if I could avoid it
I would never tell you anything

"But there's always that tension
of being burdened with 'I'"

there are two crazy trees in your eyes

the first time he burned the town
it fell like a grove of
giant chrysanthemums

the second time he burned the town
green stagnant water
came between his teeth

the third time he burned the town
his fingers were filled with
white chrysanthemums

the first time he burned the town
he hated himself
and he hated the town

the second time he burned the town
he loved himself
though he hated the town

there was no third time he burned the town

THE ROOM

[1]

When Jesse moved to another neighborhood my father drove me to her house for a sleepover. In the twilight that stretched out and out I turned away from myself. Standing in front of the mirror in Jesse's room I tried to tie the tie Abby, Jesse's mother, had given me to wear. Then Abby came into the room; she reached for the light switch without quite reaching it. I stood there rooted to the floor as though I were a tree, staring at her beauty as though she were a tree. Abby looked the way Jesse would look someday. I held the point of my tie in my fingers in the sunlight and I saw her hair in the sunlight. I was ten. Now the rain pops against the window, somewhere twigs click against the window of a room, somewhere the wind breaks into a roar like an ocean. My eyelids popped open two hours ago. One window fills with milky violet, the other with slate gray. I transform everyone into my family; Greg and Mark Thienpont were like my brothers: Mark once said he wanted to trade mothers with me. When he said that his face looked hopeful, and I was attracted to their hot-tempered mother, Ingrid, a woman from Germany. The human body extends toward the radiance only we can embody. When I was seven and Mark must have been almost five a bunch of kids were racing bikes in the alley. I was coming from one direction and Mark was coming from the opposite direction. I didn't swerve even though my bicycle was heading straight for his. My bike was larger so when we crashed I fell farther, free of the bikes. Mark was crying with his foot caught in the spokes. Fourteen years later, when I got fired from a bookstore, I called my parents and they told me Mark had been killed the day before in a car crash in a sudden rain. He wasn't driving: he had been caddying at a country club: he was just catching a ride home.

[11]

Last night I was alive, scared pointless, waiting.
Darkness hugged me in the room where I wrote
about my mother. Our split nerves react alike.
When her uncle was a boy he was made to stand
watching the Cossacks as they killed his mother.

I talk to Jane (safe Jane),
the only one at the party who will
talk to me for more than three
sentences and not then
look away and act bored.

I start to think, "Oh,
all they're doing is ego-
airing: everyone at this party
is just saying, I do this
I do that, I
sleep with her I
sleep with him,
I'm going to be this,
I'm going to be that."

[III]

I'm afraid of what I'd write if I wrote today. It's stupid to try to talk about this: I can't write about my fear of writing badly; I can't write about my fear of admitting my own depression. Or can I? I sit around for hours and hours doing nothing: on a windy spring day I sit on a park bench on Commonwealth Ave. writing this. Lightning runs across the street. There is no moment when everything suddenly looks the way it does now. I desire too many women because I am stale and afraid. Desire spins like water in the sink flashing on the porcelain. Lightning runs across the street. Now she's standing at the bus stop in blue and pink cotton, in her tan, in her lovely self-absorption. I'm stale and afraid—face up to it; I stare at the camera, trying to face up to it. Nothing makes sense to me but I trust these words will come out right. I trust you will understand. I know you cannot save me. You might ask: "Who is you? Do you mean me?" When we fight the way we did last weekend I wish I could mean someone besides you. I wish I could stop writing love poems. I need to look closely at what I've become at this moment. Well, I have eight legs and an exoskeleton, my eyes are livid taupe, and in each mandible I hold a tiny, screaming baby.

[IV]

I spit dirt from my numb mouth. I refuse to let myself hate you.

He drifted on the water, in the sunlight,
Afraid of the light, afraid of the water.
He floated on his back with his eyes shut
Until he couldn't remember:

Which direction is the shore?

On the sharp blue ocean the speedboat jolts down and forward.
We watch from the deck of the ferry where we're hit
By spray in the cold wind. A black hole has opened
Beneath me and I do not know what to feel.

I see currents and angles as facets within the moving skin of the water.
When I floated on my back I listened to my breathing
And it didn't sound right; it sounded warped.
The water is a moving table. Even though you're going to

Leave me I feel good with your arms around me.
You say, "I'm getting kind of dizzy looking through this grating"
As the ferry pitches forward, then backward,
Then forward again like the rhythm of sick breathing.

Living with me must have been like watching that boy
Leaning over the railing, licking the clear, shiny spray off his hand.

The Room

On the hottest night you changed the voice you had.

I am too simple, I flatten
These words and these seconds

Destroyed by my voice, a fraud
Talking into the heat.

We walked up our tangled kite string.

Flailing my arms, I float away from you and
You watch me float away.

Nothing in the room
Belongs in the room.

Our tangled kite string, and no kite.

You open the floor and go outside: in this, the sound
Of a heartbeat, in this, in this.

It didn't happen here nor could it
When it happened.

The hottest night of the summer, afraid that no one.

Your voice reaches me, filling our room
Not to fill the room but to leave the room.

Stable and afraid,
You opened the hardwood floor.

CRYSTAL ROCK

1.

The sun drills a hole between my shoulder blades
I am ashamed that I want self-degrading things
I burn for no reason like a lantern in daylight

Do I believe in evil?
To commit a sin you have to intend
To commit a sin

The pleasures that I need contradict each other

Weeds and grass stab through flat shining water
When I step on them to cross the black mud
The cold water shakes, distorting flat branches

My back muscles pull tight
Like string being tied in a knot
Come here and pull me
Tighter and tighter

2.

Snow covers the slope
and long ice patches stick out
where the stream has frozen.
The ice looks almost blue.
Branches balance
against one another
to form structures
resembling walls or huts.
In the cold we hear the
wind start in the pines.

One footstep will be
padded by the snow,
the next will crunch
and pack the snow hard.
When I slide my fingers
over your fingers
I feel time—
more than four years
since I first stroked your hand.
We feel so much pleasure
that I'm afraid.
The sky is oatmeal-colored,
thick and near.
Beige-yellow leaves,
curled into spirals,
clatter on twigs
in the cold wind.
At Crystal Rock,
with the fields and barns
spread beneath us,
we press the pine needles
against our cheeks.

3.

I reach straight up like an oak tree
heat flows in the strong branch
the moon shines in the freezing sky
the moon shines on the branch

need breathing need

in my stomach
there is
a chunk of agate
the motion rushing forward
in your stomach
slams you into me

wide open
without pain
every nerve in your body pulses
open yet still
opening

sun heat is pulsing inside you
you bump against the branch
your hand reaches, cups the moon
shining on the tight branch

ride the sun inside the branch
create me and teach me
you feed me from your big, full
churning smile

ride the sun inside the branch
moving your whole body
back and forth squeezing heat

I breathe like an oak tree
I taste your sweating skin
in my mouth and your sweat
moistens my eyes with heat

knowledge shines in your voice; knowledge
pushes your rhythm

we laugh in the dark

each of us sets the rhythm
urging the other on
each of us takes pleasure

I reach straight up like an oak tree
heat flows in the strong branch
the moon shines in the freezing sky
the moon shines on the branch

sun heat is pulsing inside you
moving your whole body;
you squeeze the pulsing heat

your moist hair and your skin
smell like the earth during rain
sun heat is pulsing inside you
here is the river in the sun

I CAN NO LONGER LIVE BY THINKING

My hands breathe new tightening inside the branch, inside the branch. You are everything I don't know. I think I dreamed this before or maybe I lived through it. You throw me through my skull. The wet moon. There is nothing to be afraid of. You throw me—I need to go there—I need to breathe. Nothing to be afraid of. My hands breathe new the branch because of the violence with which you force me to breathe. Sometimes I'm afraid of everything. Throw me through my skull. The ground rises in my throat—I'm going to hit the ground. Green seedlings flip and twist. My hands breathe new tightening inside the branch, inside the branch.

when we kiss you force me to breathe

THE SUN DRENCH

for Kimberley Gavin

1.

Nerves torn to shreds,
in the red clusters

hanging from twigs
in the rain.

I was in need,
but also saying stop.

Bright red berries, mucus-slick, scattering
and bobbing on the water.

I stay in need, wide open,
not knowing how to stop,

begging you, claiming
I have outrun my anger.

2.

Thaw reaches up
through water shining on mud.

We feel heat in the branches,
wide open, loving what we feel.

Thaw reaches up through mud,
drenching wet opens stink,

stains concrete moss-colored.
Will you make a seed

sprout in our palms,
make the wood floor in sunlight

a blanket on fire?
We stand in the wet

reaching for each other, opposite
directions, where we are.

3.

Sunlight changes the water
to green-yellow between the rocks

where a red leaf clenches.
Thaw rises from the

hard packed mud
in sun sheets

rising near the birches'
shining white bark,

their bared outline.
Wind starts, the walls

and the wood floor
shimmer in the sun drench.

4.

The water on the ground
shines, a polished spoon.

You jump all nets,
up and up, each phrase

a stamen between petals'
glistening, buoyant argument.

You gesture, "We will stop,
but stay near me."

You fold flannel sheets,
pack them in a cardboard box,

shake fire-colored wool
across our hardwood floor.

Through a tree trunk coated in wet
your words push,

my breathing in a branch
standing straight up.

5.

You taught me our happiness,
sun heat in the branches.

Standing straight up,
I moved under your weight,

caressing your strength.
Buds swelled, red berries

sweetened, our truth spilled
into sound, love cries

opening again.
Long pleasure, wood

breathing heat in our legs.
When we fumble and trust

friendship, kid my self-pity,
salve me with laughter.

HIGHER GROUND

There is a scrap of foam rubber on the sidewalk in front of the yellow coin-operated newspaper rack with *Boston Herald* in red paint; behind the piece of foam rubber, in the shadow of the newspaper rack, is a grimy napkin. It's not nearly as bad as a picture of a mutilated hand seconds after the hand got caught in a threshing machine. Why do I think of the hand? Drink something cold; feel the wind blow into your shirt and cool your skin. Then I think, "The torn skin, the punctured skin," but my skin is not torn or punctured, and I stand here feeling the sunlight and the wind. The picture of the mutilated hand is more real than the sunlight and the wind.

In the middle of nowhere I look at a picture of Kim and me taken five years ago. In the picture we are sitting close to each other staring straight ahead. Now she is asleep and I'm sitting near her tearing out my hair. Before she fell asleep she told me to stay near her. I open a notebook from two summers ago and find this: "Why is degradation a comfort? Because you know you have sunk as far as you can? No. There is a moment, faint as if touched in sleep, when you feel yourself transgressing, crossing over the line into the forbidden. You feel something give way, and that feels safe—a respite from the expectation you have for yourself that you are, or can be, or should be, 'good.'"

The notebook asks, Do you have a world? I cannot say that I have only one world. I would like to—

These words tell the truth but they are flimsy and brittle attempts to hide.

I look at someone for a second and start to imagine that I am him, then I see my reflection in a window and my identity comes back in horror. In front of the convention center they have set up a "trout pool." They have transported clean water and big trout from somewhere in the countryside and they are letting people fish for ten minutes per person in a low, rectangular sky-blue wading pool. A chunky guy with no shirt on carries one bucket of live trout after another from the truck to the pool. The trout are stunned for a second or two after he dumps them into the water, then they start to swim back and forth. It's a promotion for a company that makes fishing line. I hear a little girl say, "Trout look like tadpoles."

I sat on the ledge near the lawn in front of a department store. The wind swept down from the black sky, I should have worn a jacket. No one walked by while I ate the peanuts and drank the grapefruit juice. I wanted to go to the Pour House for a drink but I didn't want to be there by myself; I wanted to be near people flirting and laughing but I was afraid. Construction workers stood around a pit in the street, their faces and shoulders lit up by the lights on the roadblocks. I didn't let myself look at them. I wanted to be released.

Life is a series of shocks and injuries during which it is necessary to dress well, said Jack.

I said, Why am I even walking these streets? Once I wrote I am so afraid of being torn apart but now I can say I have been torn apart.

That is a cliché, said Jack. Really your whole stance of precious self-regard, your whole delicacy and force, is a cliché at this point. No one cares. You're just one more sensitive subjectivity in a world of unemployable wanna-be's.

Then he stood on his chair and immediately five really handsome men and five really handsome women surrounded him. They chanted, "We will be your community. We will be your community."

Really, Jack turned to me and whispered, really, the thing you need is, you need a community; but you aren't going to get one because you're the last romantic individualist, or not even the last. Puppies like you are a dime a dozen. You're so boring you should be on TV. The ten laughed.

I said, I'll laugh at your jokes if you laugh at mine.

You have no sense of humor, Jack said. You don't even know how to wear a shirt. He said, You have to know how to sit in a chair and be outside the law. You have never known and you will never know.

The next night I came back to the bar but I stayed in the shadows. Well, I'm afraid. Well, don't go outside. As soon as I go outside I'm in five streets at once. This is wonderful, I can see five different views at once. I go back inside—nothing has changed: I realize there is only one direction I can go and that is forward. Just as I walk onstage Jack, smirking like a game show host, walks onstage holding giant quotation marks made of painted blue cardboard. He is saying, Folks, folks, stop me if you've heard this one before.

You heard your voice say, "I am often afraid of madness."

Think back over everything she said, everything that started you thinking everything would be all right, everything would be good, the way things were going was good, and things would just keep going that way.

Now at least you can see that nothing good can last, or it feels that way right now.

"I am often afraid
of madness."

Think back over everything she said, everything that you can remember, and try to remember everything you thought: what you thought about the future, what you thought about getting through each day, what you thought about the apartment.

"I am often afraid of madness": you heard your voice say that so you thought it was true.

You walked through the city on a day when you had a million things to do, things you should have been doing, but instead you walked from bookstore to bookstore looking for some book you had purchased a long time before but had never read, and then you sold it and then you wanted it back.

The plane has taken off; I have taken off; we have taken off; separated from the city, I look down through the night sky at the gnarl of streets. Ten days later: sunlight on the sidewalk, on water and yellow leaves; on a cement ledge parallel to the sidewalk there is a plastic cup full of beer with cigarette butts floating and, floating in the center of the cup, a red and white cotton hair-tie: I look away fast because it looks like false teeth floating in a cup of piss.

ORIENT POINT

Wavelets sound like sheets flapping.
A crab leg, just the leg, has gotten hold
Of a periwinkle. The top half of a crab shell,
Thin as enamel glaze, burnished ivory flecked

With purple, rough ovals, half ovals, squiggles.
The shell, translucent, has been cracked off
At the bottom. Green hair follicles
Are concentrated around the holes where the face once was.

The ocean, sage- and smoke-colored.
Dirty tidepools up where cars drive through.
A milk-thin clamshell striped the brown of roots:
The rounded hinge inside

Looks like a bone inside a human ear
And the periwinkle no bigger
Than a hazelnut in my palm
Gives black, wet invitations to the tongue.

Mussels, still closed, alive, hold tight
To the oozy sand, their green beards trail beside them
In wetness, glinting. The water now riled suede,
A black cormorant flying.

He wasn't really
There; my father
Was there but not
There. He hugged me
But I felt myself
Becoming resistant
In his arms.

Ben thinks of me
As part of him.
I am my poetry.
He wants me to
Be like him.
I think of his book
On voice in
American fiction,
His professorial wit.
Charming my friends,
He gives keen
Attention to a
Grad student
Who reminds
Him of himself.
He hugged me
Tight. I did not
Fight, I let him
Hug me,
Giving to me
What he could,
All he could, more
Than I could take.

I always want to say I'm sorry.
Wet sores that won't scab.

Angles in water shave lace,
Turning light.

He chooses his distance
From me with precision,

Then, suddenly charming,
He tries to make us comfortable.

So unseen by him I felt ashamed.
Unclench my hand.

Red-brown, jade, violet,
Round and bulging stones,

Cracked and ribbed,
Ocher-spotted: is my face

Divided? We were fishing;
My father slipped

On sharp rocks,
Broke, shock and pain broke out,

Did he shriek?
He stood, furious

With me, not with me.

Alter Liskofsky came from a village near Bialystok.
When nothing is taught or learned our past drains,
At Coney Island, he swam between floating ice chunks.
Fidgeting in mind, and you had better hope for magic,
A crashing family, a collapsing box:
An object, maybe some kind of wood box
Nightmare makes a groping tunnel;
Or a ring to heal nightmare into worth.
Did he see the New Jerusalem, awaken

After his son Stephen's death my father
Sick of poverty and shame, was he afraid
"Almost broke down . . . for years . . ."
To look up? What was this new place?
Ben hid Stephen and his other children from me
Alter could read Yiddish but not English;
Until I was fourteen: how can I write what Ben can't say?
Masha could not read at all; they spoke a patois
What did he want at twenty? His face blurs,
Of Yiddish and English, wanted the children to speak English:
He sees the world of his father as sentimental,
How did Ben talk to his parents, or to himself?
Words he loves but can't believe, a string of gutted hope.
Alter moved the family from apartment to apartment

To sneak past rent he owed.

A log in the surf looks like the dorsal fin and back
Of a bottlenose dolphin, floating. Another crab shell,
Moss-crusted green, its eye sockets are still
In place, nib-sized stalks that twist up, then snap off.

They didn't speak for I don't know
How many years. Ben looks away, "My father
Was distant from us; I don't remember much,
But one thing I remember, he loved

The ocean, we always lived near the ocean."

NEW WORLD

They stood on the shore
or that is how we
picture them, standing
on the shore. Our
nightmare makes a perfect
tunnel. We depress
each century inside
a collapsing accordion,
a crashing box on fire;
fire braids our faces.
They stood on the shore,
or we picture them
standing on the shore.
They mistook us for
gods. We are not
the us in that sentence
we insist, we beg.

MARATHON HOUSE

1.

This is what I see. Do you want to hear a voice saying this is what I see? Do I want to speak a voice saying this is what I see? This is what I see.

Men and women drift in and out of the bar, a little tipsy. Their big and sweaty motions embody desire through the muggy night. I watch them pass me while I stand at the pay phone.

A young woman wearing a plaid shirt says, "By the time I'm thirty I'll own my own business."

Nine years ago in Berkeley: I walked past a gas station and saw a woman pumping gas into her vintage sedan with fins; her boyfriend was sitting in the car combing his hair and she was wearing ankle-high boots.

The night sky, a color from an album cover. Is it wonderful or stupid that I carry this picture in my heart?

She reminded me of a friend who got hurt in New York; I just wanted to see her happy.

2.

I wanted to be an assassin. I wanted to see angels and hear them speak commands. I wanted to live in a clear trance, to be certain of the absolute truth.

There is a detective, he was there: he followed me through the streets of my hometown. He drove me out of my hometown. He followed me through the streets and made me fear my own hometown, the streets lined with elm trees and wooden houses.

If I make a promise, they nail it to the floor.

I wanted to be an assassin, with the night sky in my eyes, with a sparrow in my eyes: I wanted to pass through walls, to appear silently, and kill.

I was sitting on the steps of the Cathedral of St. John the Divine. A woman in a torn fur coat and a wig came up to me. In a second I noticed all her fingers were stumps.

3.

Nine years ago, on the rooftop in dawn air, Michelle holding me with her strong legs, her laughter and her smile changing: she says, "Your body is so free but your voice isn't."

The sign showing a muscular woman: "Inside every woman is a Goddess"—but do I believe there's a God inside every man? Is he a strict father or Jesus Christ, a seductive boy, a learner, Eros? Compassion at best.

Or is he always faking, predatory?

Last night you were standing with your friend and you started to squeeze a splinter out of your finger; as it came out it turned into a long needle; you kept squeezing and it hurt more and more and it turned into a clear worm.

4.

A ten-year-old boy playing with the other kids on the block deep into the summer evening: I want to say, Everything is still possible for that boy. That's not true but it is true; I want to be that boy.

Standing in the parking lot of Ames in Providence waiting for Donna to get through the line; I had been looking for automotive touch-up paint for my mountain bike. A thin rain, less than a drizzle—

The boy knows whether he is popular. Does he know whether he will be popular? Does he know why a woman will love him? Does he think his father is masculine enough? Does he think his friend's father is more of "a winner"?

"By the time I'm thirty I'll own my own business—"

A thin rain, less than a drizzle, and volunteers at a table near the door of Ames solicit donations to something called Marathon House. A home for recovering addicts? Tonight a girl, unmistakably upper-middle-class, who couldn't be more than fifteen, asked for any spare change.

5.

You told me you can't forget the night you stood on your front porch and tried to scream as his hand closed over your mouth. You were meant for, then, something you never meant for yourself; he meant it for you and finally you could yank your face free of him and scream.

You try sticking to friendship and throwing elegant dinner parties; you excel at this and this confirms your suspicion. Only by giving to others can you be wonderful and not get punished immediately.

A row of bright flags moving like sidewinders, open to the wind as the mouth of a sail—

Maybe life is one disaster after another, and—

6.

The bars and the diner, the friendships in this town, something even makes me think of the rosebushes my father used to grow alongside the garage. He says he might start them again. Past the road, past the furniture warehouse, past yellow cattails in a field, standing water answers the sky with more questions.

Kids sit on benches, couples greet each other, walking. Families gather, hand drinks out, fathers look at sons who will graduate soon. Family likeness, family weakness, family dwelling; housewife, household, hold back, back out: you wanted me like you.

Pink suds fleck the pond surface, a bubble bath of chemical runoff. Somehow these cement bricks stacked up are the ground for knowing anything.

Trees at the edge of the marsh, water greener than leaves, marsh grass, flat, hair-thin: marriages, journeys to witness promises broken and then, strangely, fixed.

7.

After I mopped the floor and restocked the milk machine I sat down in front of the café with Alan, who had stopped by to talk as I closed.

Two cars, one right behind the other, at first I thought they were racing; the car behind sped up suddenly and hit the back of the car in front—just tapped it—I remember thinking, "He did that on purpose"; both cars slowed, drifted under the El tracks, and pulled over past the clothing store on the next block.

When the woman screamed I said, "Let's go"; Alan said, "We should call the police"; I said, "You call the police."

I ran as fast as I could and when I was under the El tracks I thought, "What if he has a gun? What if there are lots of them?" and then I thought, "I'll think of something."

I came out from under the El tracks and I could see his car parked behind hers, both driver's-side doors were open.

The woman trying to fight him off, hitting him and trying to push him out of the front seat of her car.

Without breaking stride, I yelled, "Let her go," yelling from far down in my chest, commanding. I kept running and he let her go and got out of her car and ran back to his; I was still a hundred yards away. She started to get out of her car and he drove straight at her and then past her and away.

When I reached her and comforted her and we were both saying the license plate number over and over, lights were starting to go on in apartments.

8.

Say I love you, I love. Say it means what it means. She said, "Your body is so free but your voice isn't—"

The small green bush trembles in the wind. Everything is going away, but the wind is moist and warm. I glance up at the old clock on the wall, a big green flower with twelve yellow plastic petals.

Donna, are we in the old wet leaves and new straw, in harvest bows I see on the doors of houses as I walk? Are we in the voices in the supermarket? Is it in darkness in the corners of the room, darkness under our bodies, darkness between your breasts? I love how much you want to be with me, and that you believe our lives can be ordinary and full.

This is not what I want to say but the cold spins inside of me and then spins out again like a web. This is not what I meant to say but it makes a mark in black paint on white canvas.

Used books piled in cardboard boxes outside another lousy restaurant; a steel sky. Just another neighborhood with no money, where two writers can afford to live, no real community.

Everything is going away, taking part of us with it, leaving part of us behind. Night beginning, and people hurry to whatever they have, and there's nothing here, I don't know anyone here. The window shines; the sky streaks a clay blue stain.

Why is what is going away everything? Why is it everything? But there is so much left here, so the word *nothing* glows as brightly as the night sky. A negative angel, a paradox, the stars burning in the night sky.

The small green bush trembles in the wind. Cars leave oil streaks on the street.

"FOOTLOOSE RADISH . . ."

Footloose radish

captivating wave after wave of
pleasure,

tell me you will shake this broom.

Dust my wave. The broom
brushes away the footprints and the house turns and
waves.

Ocean, much laughter,
the broom moving by itself.

Who gave back shadows on the snow, green-
brown water rising through cracked thick ice,
a wave

in slow motion?

Radishes, turpentine, broom on the wall
near the back stairs that lead

to waves of wet dark.

The loom in time is broom
earned.

Wave hello,
turn into shimmering footprints, dust my broom

and the whole outstanding tale.

JOSEPH LEASE has published his poems widely in such magazines as *Grand Street, The Paris Review, Southwest Review, Pequod, Colorado Review, The Boston Review,* and *Agni.* He was educated at Columbia, Harvard, and Brown, where he completed his M.F.A. in poetry. A winner of the Academy of American Poets Prize, Joseph Lease lives in Boston. *The Room* is his first collection of poems.

Designed and typeset in Adobe Caslon 10/13 by
Erik Rieselbach for Flying Lead Changes, New York.
Printed on Monadnock Dulcet by
Becotte & Gershwin, Warminster, Pennsylvania

Alef Books are published in association with
the Educational Alliance, Inc.,
New York.